A Parent's Guide To Signs of Gang Involvement

By: Author Randy Cochran

<u>About the Book:</u>

This book is intended to help parents identify signs that their child may be in a gang. It will also assist parents in keeping their child from joining a gang.

Author Cochran will share his past as a gang leader with you. He considers himself to be a gang expert, one who never went to Harvard, or Yale. The streets where he lived the gang life, from age ten to his mid forty's, were his college. Author Cochran is no longer a gang member, he now lives his life helping young people avoid going down the same path he went down.

He wants parents to use this book as a guide to help keep their kids from joining a gang and if they are in a gang, a guide to how to get help before it's too late.

Dedications:

This book is dedicated to all the parents who have lost a child or loved one to gang violence.

Acknowledgements:

Special thanks to Bianca Storey for helping me prepare myself to write this story and for joining me as the COO of Heartbeat Don Publications. It feels good to see my dream of being the CEO/owner of this company come true and it has made me humble to know I have people depending on me to take care their family.

Also, special thanks to Katrina Breier for giving

me advise and being on my side no matter what, you are a true friend.

To my mom Barbara Cochran, who did all she could do to keep me out of the streets. Like so many other kids, I let the money and cars get the best of me. You did your part Mom, love you 4 ever, 2 die-4.

Shout out to my Heartbeat Team, Dawn Trigg, Ollie Vail, Tammy Cochran, Tina Thomas, Shadreka Thomas, Auntie Jackie Thomas, my dad what's up, Clarence Edward Thomas, my sister-Wee-Wee, Cornelia Thomas, Shani Vail, Shaquana Cochran Amber Cochran Stephanie Thomas Davon Thomas, man hold it down you and Tyren Thomas. This year going to be better, I'm doing my thing. What's popping? Sheveran Hardy, Sam-Dog, 808, Bozack, Germaine Leggett, Ricky Santiago Sr., John Scully (Ice man), Jerry Santingo Sr., Maya Washington, Melissa Easley, Sheldon Gaynor, Domique Storey. What's good? Free my man "Buck" Aka Kenny Hardy, love ya bruh!

Author Notes:

Shout out to my football team- D-buildings in the house!! Champs!! In fact let me say this hands down, no one on Autry State Prison compound hit harder than me with that pad…, Facts!

Shout out to the wardens at Autry State Prison, shout out to the Recreation Department, thanks for the football and basketball. To all the Recreation Aids, "man I'm sorry if I lose my cool sometimes, but I work with you all every day. Sports in prison is just a past time.

My title is Author Randy Cochran, Owner/CEO of Heartbeat Don Publications. I'm not saying this to brag, because I am a humble person. I'm letting you all know that if I can do it, you can do it! No matter what, don't stop pushing for better.

Shout out to my main man, Miami Fat, Big smokes, J-Roker AKA big Will, to a special friend who need to be free. Horace 'Jack' Sparks, shout out to my man Raimone 'Red Dog' Boyaton, Kenny Sir Phive' Jackson, John C Davis, Ricardo Cartledge AKA Jihad, Chavez, Schoolboy G, Andre 'Dre' Bowman, Donta Brown, Carina Styles, 'Bally'- Kassie Smith, Miami-(380) No hard feelings, man I love you like a little brother.

Special thanks to a man that I have the upmost respect for. A man who has been around a long time, who has a lot of knowledge, wisdom and understanding. A man who has helped a lot of brothers get out of prison no matter what their color is, this man has been part of the Civil Right movement, Mr. Andre McCrary. Thank you for being part of the Heartbeat Freedom Team, we love and respect you and we thank you congressman John Lewis.

Prologue:

A little bit about the Author's past:

Hello, my name is Randy Cochran. I was raised in Connecticut, in the city of Hartford, in one of the worst projects on the North end; Stowe Village, AKA Crookville. My mom had three boys and three girls. Being raised by my mother as a single parent, it was hard for me to stay in sports but my favorite sport was boxing.

My mom always kept it real with me, she used to tell me, "Son, it's easy to get in trouble, but it's hard to get out. Now watch who you hang around!" That went in one ear and out the other. I did just what my mother told me not to do. I started hanging with guys who got in trouble and then I started getting in trouble myself. Come to find out, my new friends were part of a gang. All the time I was hanging with them their plan was to recruit me into the gang.

The older guy, who was the leader, would send me out to fight. They would set matches up for me and bet money on me, which the leader would pay me if I won. They saw I could fight so they gave me some rules and made me part of there gang at the tender age of ten!

My mom knew something was not right. She use to question me all the time and I would lie and say, "No Mom, I am not in a gang!" I started failing in school, wearing different color clothes and I started having run in's with law enforcement. My attitude changed, I became more aggressive.

Then one day in school, a big gang fight broke out. Stowe Village vs Albany Ave. I was suspended from school and that's when my mom really knew I was a young gang member. I was sent to Juvenile for fighting, but that didn't stop me. I started carrying a gun at the age of twelve.

My mom did all she could do to keep me away from the gangs. One summer she had a plan, she sent me down South, to Georgia. I stayed with my uncle for a while, but trouble seemed to find me. In the end, I ended up going to prison for murder. I lost everything; my family and my friends, no one cared what happened to me. My mom and Aunt Margaret Cochran, AKA Moot were all I had. They didn't have much to give me as far as money, but they did show me unconditional love.

When I came into the Georgia prison system I weighed 165 lbs. but growing up in a gang, on the streets, it was easy for me to upgrade and join right in. I was already a black gangster disciple.

I went to prison and joined the Organization for Growth and Development (GD) and I became one of the biggest leaders in Georgia Prison. For 22 years I led the (GD's) at over 17 different prisons in Georgia, including all level five prisons that were considered the most dangerous.

I retired from the gang life and I have no ties to the Organization of Growth and Development (GD), my life is now dedicated to teaching youth and helping parents identify the signs of being in a gang.

I consider myself a gang expert, not because I've been to college and studied from a textbook, but because at the age of ten I was experiencing and living what professor's and so-called gang counselor's make millions to tell you about. Most people who talk about gangs have never been in a gang, they teach you about what they read in a book.... Well this book is authentic and I pray that kids, parents, young adults, doctors, lawyers and correctional institutions everywhere, can understand more about gangs in America through its pages.....

<u>A gang is…</u>
<u>A group of youths who identify each other with signs, symbols or colors.</u>

- Most gang members are age 12-23.
- Ninety percent of all gang members in the US are male.
- About 46 percent are Hispanic.
- 34 percent African American.
- 12 percent are Caucasian.
- 8 percent are Asian or of another ethnicity.

Gang Activity is no longer confined to a few, large, inner cities. Gangs have been documented in every state in the United States and are active in rural and suburban communities, as well as Urban Areas.

How do I know if my child is in a Gang?

Parents should be aware of the following warning signs that may indicate gang involvement…

> - Shirts, hats and other clothing of specific colors.
> - Gang graffiti.
> - Unexplained money.
> - Caring of guns or knives.
> - Gang tattoos.

Note:

Parents should also look for changes in behavior, such as poor or failing grades in school, a hostile or defiant attitude, drugs or alcohol use, involvement in illegal activities or trouble with law enforcement.

What Can I do to prevent my child from joining a gang?

- ➤ Listen to your child. Many youth turn to gangs because they don't think they can trust or confide in anyone else.
- ➤ Build a strong relationship with your child.
- ➤ Show them love and attention.
- ➤ Communicate positive messages.
- ➤ Let your child know you care about them, believe in him/or her and accept them.
- ➤ Help them identify what their talents are.
- ➤ Direct your children toward healthy activities and find ways for them to be successful at what they enjoy.
- ➤ Praise them for their accomplishments and always make sure that they understand how important they are to your family.

What Factors Contribute to Gang Affiliation?

Specific social conditions can place young people at risk for gang involvement.

- ➢ Living in poverty- gangs provide a source of income.
- ➢ Living in a community that lacks jobs and organized activities for youth such as after school sports, YMCA and Scouts.
- ➢ Having other family members in gangs.
- ➢ Living in a neighborhood where gangs are present.
- ➢ Low self-esteem, or feelings of isolation.
- ➢ Inconsistent or ineffective parenting, such as lack of family rules.
- ➢ Ineffective discipline, no monitoring of youth activities.

Note:

Young boys and girls in these situations often see gangs as a way out of poverty and into a community where they will be accepted and protected. They adopt negative behaviors that earn praise from the gang which perpetuates more negative behavior.

Parents and other adults should learn appropriate prevention and intervention strategies to avoid or interrupt these negative cycles.

Avoid Scare Tactics

Young people who are interested in or involved in gangs, usually won't be frightened away from their loyalties. They may see only the positive short term consequences of their actions. Calmly discuss the long term consequences and realities of gang life... Prison, serious injury and even death.

> ➤ Back up what you say with facts.
> ➤ Talk about how decisions today can affect their future.
> ➤ Find ways to occupy your children's' time. Get them involved in after school programs, Art, history, dance class, ext.
> ➤ Explore interests or hobbies that might be enjoyable and beneficial.
> ➤ Assign responsibilities at home.

Invest Quality time

- ➢ Spend time with your child.
- ➢ Plan activities that the whole family can enjoy.
- ➢ Expose your child to places beyond your neighborhood. Take them to parks, museums, beaches and to visit positive friends.
- ➢ Find out what your child likes.

Note:

Nine times out of ten if your child's friend is a gang member, your child is a gang member as well. Get to know your child's friends, encourage your child to invite his/her friends over to your house. Be a positive influence in their lives.

Should I set limits at Home?

Yes set limits at your home!

Your children need to know, at an early age, what acceptable behavior is and what unacceptable behavior is in your home. Do not allow your child to stay out late, or spend a lot of unsupervised time out in the streets. You can't control everything they do, but you can be aware of where they are and who they are with.

"Momma I should have listened."

"Sonny! Sonny! Sonny! You are late for school Sonny," Mom said.

Sharon White was a hardworking, church going woman who was a head nurse at Hartford Health Care Medical Group in South Windsor CT. Sharon moved to Windsor Connecticut after she married her husband, Benny White and had her son, Sonny, a year later. Sonny was now 17 years old and A student in school. Sharon's husband was killed in the Army ten years ago and Sharon was left to raise her son alone. She dated a few times, but most of her days were spent serving the Lord. She helped the church feed the homeless and was also a Sunday school teacher.

Sonny was part of the church and played drums

for the choir. But lately Sharon had to get onto Sonny for hanging with a boy named Bruce, her spirit just did not set well when it came to him. Sharon always thought Bruce was in a gang, but when she asked him he would say no, he was not a gang member, Sharon had no way to tell if he was lying, she knew nothing about gangs.

One day Sharon woke Sonny up and said, "You're going to be late for school. You are also have not been doing what you're supposed to be doing around the house."

Sonny replied, "Ok Mom I will take care of it.

Sharon told him, "You need to stop hanging around Bruce Hines, he's trouble and he looks like a gang member."

Sonny retorted, "Mom you say everyone looks like a gang member. Bruce is not in a gang, he would have told me."

"Ok, one day you going to wish you had listened to me," Sharon said.

Sonny went out the door and waited on the bus to take him to Capital Preparatory Magnet School.

When Sonny got on the bus, Bruce Hines was in the back. He always held Sonny a seat next to him. Bruce had on all black, with a black flag hanging out the right side of his back pocket, Sonny was too lame to know what that meant, he was just a true friend to Bruce, no matter what his mom or Pastor Jones, who his mom had told to talk to him, said.

Bruce said, "What's good folks?"

Sonny replied, "Chilling man."

Bruce said, "Man we going to have some fun tonight. There's a party downtown Hartford, at the center and everyone is going to be there. "You going?"

Sonny exclaimed, "Hell yeah! Mom went to work and won't be home until after 3am."

Bruce said 'It's all good."

Bruce was from Hartford Connecticut, raised in Chapel Garden. His dad was in prison, serving life for killing a police officer during an armed robbery, Bruce's mom, Denise Hines, had three kids, one boy and two girls, when her baby daddy, Edward Hines, went to prison. Denise did what it took to take care her family but Bruce had been hanging out with guys twice his age. Bruce had been in a gang for over ten years, but no one knew.

Bruce met Sonny on the school bus and one day Sonny got into a fight with two gang members, but Sonny didn't know who they were. Bruce's crew were on the bus and waiting to see if Sonny would stand up for himself. If sonny did stand up for himself, Bruce and his crew would not let the two gang member's jump on him, Sonny would be on their list for recruitment.

Sonny was in the back seat when the bus stopped and two dudes got on. They walked to the back where Sonny was sitting and the big guy, Nanie AKA Block said, "Hey! Yo, you got to get up out of that seat, it's for my boy!" Block Boy Black was standing with his arms across his chest, both dudes had blue flags hanging from their pockets.

Bruce and his crew were watching on to see what Sonny was going to do. Sonny put down the book that was in his hand and said, "If your boy wants this seat tell him to come take it!" Sonny was loud enough for everyone on the bus to hear him.

Block said, "What, are you crazy?"

Sonny replied, "Yes, I am crazy, if you make me that way."

Black walked up to Sonny and that was all he remembered, Sonny hit Black in the nose and blood went everywhere. Black fell to his knees as Block got ready to hit Sonny from the back. That's when Bruce stepped up, grabbed his hand and said, "It's one on one."

Sonny beat Black pretty bad, right there in front of everyone. Bruce and Sonny had been best friends ever since.

Party Night

Downtown Hartford

The Center

One night Bruce called Sonny and said, "We're on our way to get you."

Sonny replied, "Ok I'm waiting."

"We riding in my big hommie's Benz 400 E. It's all white with gold rims," Bruce told him. He was very excited to be hanging with the gang's leader and to driving him around.

Ten minutes later, Bruce was pulling up to Sonny house. Sonny's mom was at work, she didn't get off until three in the morning, Sunny was sure he would be home by then.

Sonny had never rode in a Benz, it was nice. He

wondered who could afford a car like that. Bruce blew the horn and Sonny came out wearing all black Jordan's and a black polo t-shirt with black polo jeans. He walked to the car and got in the back seat. Bruce was driving and Ham-G was on the passenger side, talking on the cell phone. Ham-G put you in the mind of Warren Sapp.

Bruce said, "What's good folks."

Sonny replied, "Nothing, just chilling."

Bruce said, "This is Ham-G, my big hommie."

Sonny stuck his hand out and they shook hands as the car pulled away with a black Land Rover following them. Sonny was in the back seat listening to the music and enjoying his self.

They pulled up at the club, which it was crowded with people everywhere. Bruce was showing off with the Land Rover right behind him and girls from school looking and waving at him. He went around the block and parked the Benz then they all got out with about six more guys getting out of the land Rover.

Sonny could not help but notice that his whole crew had on all black and everyone had a black flag but him. He didn't know that he was in the mix of some gang members when they walked in the club with Ham-G leading the way. He had six tables waiting on them with drinks and whatever else they wanted. Everyone was having fun, they were all feeling good, smoking and drinking. Everyone but Sonny, he did not smoke or drink.

The girls were dancing all around the place, music was loud and smoke was in the air. Sonny looked around and saw a group of guys coming through the center of the crowd. They had on all blue, with blue flags hanging out of the left side of their pockets. Sonny saw two face's he remembered and was trying to think of where he knew them from when it hit him. They were the two dudes on the bus, Block and Black. Sonny had beat Black up in front of everyone.

Black looked over at Sonny with a crooked smile on his face.

Bruce and Sonny walked to the back of the club and were chilling, talking to two Puerto Rican chicks. Sonny was putting his mack down while Bruce was high on the weed.

The party was about over and everyone was making their way out the door when Black came up to Bruce and Sonny and said, "You want some more?" Black gave Sonny a hard look and pointed his finger at him as he and his crew walked out the door.

Everyone got in their cars and went their own ways. Bruce took Sonny home, who had to beat his mom home and get up in a few hours for church. Sonny did not miss church no matter how late he stayed up, Sunday was God day and he loved playing the drums in choir.

He went home and got into bed. Before he knew it, his mom was banging on his door and it was 9am already. Sonny jumped up and said, "Ok Mom, chill. I'm about to be ready."

His mom said. "And where you get all these crazy words from?" Sonny started laughing as Ms. White continued, "Pastor Jones is giving the sermon today."

Sonny replied, "I love when he preaches, it seems like he be talking to me."

Ms. White told him, "God can send you a message through other people."

"I believe that," Sonny said.

His mom then said, "The word on the streets is that Bruce is a big time gang member."

Sonny argued, "Mom, me and Bruce are best friends. He has not told me that he is in a gang."

Ms. White responded, "I'm praying for you and him both."

Sonny got dressed then he and his mother got in the car and headed to church.

Church

When Sharon White and her son, Sonny, walked in the church, everyone was looking at them because Sharon White was a God fearing woman and she loved the Lord and her Church.

Sonny went straight over to the drum set in front of the choir and started beating. This was what Sonny loved to do. He had invited Bruce to church one time but Bruce did not make it so Sonny never asked Bruce to come again.

They all got settled in as Pastor Jones got up and started preaching about love. How we should love each other and keep our faith in God. Pastor Jones said, "How can one group of men hate another group of men because of the color's they wear? How can you kill a man who has never done nothing to you? People, we need love in our hearts and the only way to get love in our heart is to find God!"

Sonny was listening and it came to him that Bruce really was in a gang and so was Block and Black. Sonny was mad at Bruce and after church he was going to find his best friend and ask him why he hadn't told him that he was in a gang. He told himself that his momma was right.

When church was over Sonny went out back and stood in the church yard, enjoying the sun and thinking about life.

Ms. White came out and asked, "You ready to go home?"

Sonny replied, "It's nice out, I think I'm going to walk over to Bruce's house."

His mom said. "Ok. You better be careful and come home before it gets too late."

Sonny grumbled, "Ok Mom, I hear you."

Sonny left the church on Main Street and started walking up Cleveland Ave, headed to Chapel Garden, to Bruce's house. He took the short cut across the school yard and was walking along with no worries when he saw a car speeding up the hill. He paid it no mind, people drive up there every day. But, he thought, this car was coming towards him. Sonny jumped back to see who was in it when the car stopped. All Sonny saw was a black face and a barrel with fire coming out of it. He felt his skin being ripped apart by bullets as he lost consciousness.

Sonny's life was playing through his mind in reverse. He was at the church, the club with Bruce, the fight on the bus with Black, he stole ten dollars from his mom's pocket book, he heard his mom crying then he was a baby and his father was playing with him.

Sonny could hear the sirens coming and a big crowd had gathered on the school yard. Word was out that a drive by shooting had just taken place. Police were everywhere questioning people. It was the 13th killing in Hartford and no one had any answers. Eyewitnesses say they saw a gray Chevy Impala speeding off.

Bruce got in his mom's car and headed to Hartford Hospital. He felt bad, Sonny was his best friend and he had never told Sonny that he was in a gang because he didn't want to run Sonny off. Bruce knew it was another gang that shot Sonny and someone was going to pay.

Sonny was rushed into surgery they worked hard to save him, he was in bad shape. Ms. White was at the hospital, along with Pastor Jones and a few other church members. Sonny had just left church when this happened and Ms. White was mad and hurt. She saw Bruce but she knew the Lord did not want her to hate. She reached out and hugged Bruce instead. She cried hard and said, "Sonny would not listen!"

Sonny stayed in surgery for hours and Ms. White stayed right there waiting. Finally a doctor came out with sweat running down his bald head and walked over to the waiting loved ones.

Ms. White ran over to him and asked, "How is my son?"

The doctor did not say anything as he wiped the sweat from his head. He finally looked up and said, "By the Grace of God, he's hanging on."

Ms. White let out a huge sigh and asked, "Can I see him?"

The doctor replied, "Yes, for a minute."

Ms. White walked in the recovery room and saw her son laying there with tubes all over him. She got down on her knees and told God, "Let Your will be done." Ms. White was crying and talking in tongue when she looked up and saw Bruce walk in.

He walked over to Sonny's bed and looked down at his best friend. Bruce whispered to Sonny saying, "Man, I'm sorry I didn't tell you that I was a gang member." He then cried for the first time in a long time. He was hurt, he loved Sonny like a brother he never had.

Ms. White was still on the floor praying when Bruce walked out of the room. On her knees praying, she asked God to let her son say another word. She wanted to hear her baby's voice. He was all Ms. White had. She got off her knees and went over to her son in bed. She grabbed his hand, held it close to her and prayed some more.

While Ms. White was prying, Sonny's eyes came open. She cried and said, "Baby it's Momma, I love you."

Sonny's mouth moved and then some barely audible words came out, "Momma, I should have listened."

Suddenly the machines went crazy and the line went flat. The doctors and nurses ran in and hurried Ms. White back to the hallway.

She and the pastor were still praying ten minutes later when the doctor came out. Everything got quiet and everyone waited to hear his words.

The doctor bowed his head and said, "I'm sorry."

Ms. White fell to her knees and sobbed. The last words she heard from her only child were, "Momma, I should have listened."

Let the story of Sonny be a lesson, you never know who you're kids are hanging

Around unless you find out. Parents make sure you know your kid's friends

Do not allow your child to hang with gang members.

May God bless you all!
Author Randy Cochran

"Parent Alert"

If you are concerned that your child might be involved in a gang, you should first talk about the situation with a school counselor, law enforcement officer or gang expert.

If a gang related incident occurs, make sure you cooperate with authorities. Your help and support may prevent others from becoming victims of gang violence.

RESOURCES

GIRLS AND BOYS TOWN NATIONAL HOTLINE

800-448-3000

24 hours • 7 Days a week • Bilingual

www.girlsandboystown.org

Free parenting help, call with any problem, anytime.

MY TROUBLED TEEN

https://www.mytroubledteen.com/SearchResult/q/Help-My-Teenage-Son-is-in-a-Gang-/

Headquarters:

1240 E 100 S Bldg 23 #204

St George, UT 84790

Phone: (866) 492-9454

Email: help@mytroubledteen.com

PARENTS' GUIDE TO GANGS

https://youth.gov/federal-links/parents%E2%80%99-guide-gangs

This resource is designed to provide parents with answers to common questions about gangs and to help them recognize and prevent gang involvement.

NATIONAL GANG CENTER

https://www.nationalgangcenter.gov/

Phone:

(850) 385-0600

(800) 446-0912

National Gang Center

Post Office Box 12729

Tallahassee, FL 32317

FBI RESOURCES

Learn to recognize the warning signs of gang involvement and get advice on bullying and other issues through:

The U.S. Department of Justice Gang Toolkit.

http://www.cops.usdoj.gov/default.asp?item=1309

Visit the FBI's Violent Gangs website for more information on the gang threat and anti-gang resources.

https://www.fbi.gov/investigate/violent-crime/gangs

GANGFREE.ORG

Gangfree.org was developed by the Gang Alternatives Program (GAP), a 501(c)(3) non-profit organization that provides services and programs to promote a gangfree lifestyle to young people and their families.

http://www.gangfree.org/gangs_child.html

Recommended Websites for further information on gang prevention and identification:

National Gang Center:

http://www.nationalgangcenter.gov/

National Youth Gang Center: http://www.iir.com/nygc

US Department of Justice:

http://www.ojjdp.gov/programs/antigang/